Christmas Programs for Children

PROGRAM RESOURCES FOR
A JOYFUL CELEBRATION

Compiled by
Elaina Meyers

Standard®
PUBLISHING
Bringing The Word to Life

Cincinnati, Ohio

Scripture taken from the HOLY BIBLE, NEW INTERNATIONAL VERSION®. NIV®.
Copyright © 1973, 1978, 1984 by International Bible Society.
Used by permission of Zondervan. All rights reserved.

Editorial team: Elaina Meyers, Rosemary H. Mitchell, Courtney Rice
Cover design: Brigid Naglich
Inside design: Bob Korth

Published by Standard Publishing
Cincinnati, Ohio
www.standardpub.com
Copyright © 2008 by Standard Publishing.
All rights reserved.

ISBN 978-0-7847-2133-9

CONTENTS

Show and Tell

Diana C. Derringer

Summary: A small child describes a nativity ornament as his show-and-tell.
Character:
  SMALL CHILD
Setting: younger elementary classroom
Costume: clothing to give appearance of a small child
Prop: nativity ornament
Running Time: 6 minutes

The SMALL CHILD shuffles to center stage very tentatively with head down, then reaches into a pocket to withdraw the nativity ornament, holds it high, takes a deep breath, and begins talking. Words are very mechanical at first, but gradually become more natural.

SMALL CHILD: This is my show-and-tell. *[points]* This is a Christmas ornament. You put ornaments on the Christmas tree. My dad always chops the tree, and my mom vacuums up the mess the tree makes. She keeps saying, "Why do we have to get a messy, old, real tree?" But my dad says it's tradition *[raises hands and shrugs shoulders]*, whatever that is.

Anyway, after my dad chops the tree and my mom cleans up the mess, then we get to put the stuff on the tree. We've got fat Santas and skinny Santas. We've got pretend candy canes and real cookies. But my mom puts some kind of stuff on the cookies, so we can't eat them. She puts the cookies on the tree every year, and they don't rot 'cause of the stuff. *[pauses, scratches head as though trying to think]* Oh yeah, we've got lots and lots of angels and fancy bows and lights. *[stops suddenly]* Uh oh, I forgot, you have to put the lights on first. Then you put on the other stuff. Anyway, we've got a bunch *[arms spread]* of stuff. I get to help if it's not the glass stuff that breaks. Mom says she doesn't need any more messes to clean up.

Mom always plays Christmas music and smiles a lot while we fix the tree, unless she sees a bug. Then she stops smiling and starts screaming, and then she tells my dad, "See, I told you we should get an artificial tree."

After my dad gets rid of the bug and my mom starts smiling again, we finish putting the stuff on the tree. The very last thing we put on the tree is this. *[holds ornament forward with a stiff arm]* This is called a nativity scene. I don't exactly know what the word *nativity* means, but *[points and looks closely]* see these three people in the middle? Well, this little one in a manger is baby Jesus. He's just been born. This woman is His mommy; her name is Mary. And this man is Joseph. The reason they are out here with these animals is they couldn't find a motel room, even though they tried and tried. *[looks up and smiles broadly]* I think it would be cool to sleep out there, but I don't think my mom would like it.

Anyway, after Jesus was born and they wrapped Him up, these guys with sheep showed up, 'cause a bunch of angels scared 'em almost to death singing all of a sudden in the sky, telling them about Jesus being born. But one angel said *[in a loud voice]*, "Fear not!" After he told them the Savior, Jesus, was born, the sheep guys decided they had to see this with their own eyes.

Now, these guys over here with the crowns and treasure chests and stuff—my mom says they shouldn't really be there 'cause they had to come from a long way away and it prob'ly took them at least two or three years to find Jesus. *[frowns and wrinkles forehead]* Man, they must've really wanted to see Him bad to take that long looking for a baby.

Anyway, they followed this star up here. *[points]* Well, actually not *this* star, but the star in the sky that showed them where Jesus was. I'm not sure why they put these guys on the same ornament if they weren't even there 'til Jesus was prob'ly walkin'. *[pauses while looking closely]* Oh well, anyway that's what my mom says.

But the reason we put this ornament on last is because it's the most important one. My mom and dad say Christmas ain't *[pauses and makes a face]*, *isn't* about getting presents, even if that is a lot of fun. Christmas isn't even about Santa Claus or Frosty or Rudolph or any of those guys. It's about Jesus being born as the Savior of the world. So this ornament goes on last, right out in front of the tree so we don't forget and so we can tell people when they come.

Do you want to hear what my mom taught me to help me remember this story? *[pauses]* OK, here goes. *[gently lays ornament to the side, clears throat, stands at attention, and puts hands behind back]*

I bring you good news of great joy that will be for all the people. Today in the town of David a Savior has been born to you; he is Christ the Lord. (Luke 2:10-11)

[relaxes body] And that's why this ornament is so important. *[smiles broadly, picks up ornament, and exits with an occasional skip]*

The Reason We Celebrate

Darlene Mitchell

Summary: The two narrators are trying to find out if anyone still remembers the true reason why we should celebrate Christmas. After interviewing several people and getting many reasons why Christmas is celebrated, one stranger finally tells the biblical reason why we should be celebrating.

Characters:
NARRATOR 1
NARRATOR 2
WOMAN 1
WOMAN 2
CHILD
WOMAN 3
HOMELESS MAN
MEAN MAN
WISE MAN

Setting: The play takes place in an outside scene in the midst of all the Christmas shoppers. All characters except the two narrators are frozen until it's their turn to speak. Once a character finishes speaking, he stands motionless again.

Props: old blanket, ball, department store shopping bags, grocery store bags, cell phone, quarter, Bible

Running Time: 20 minutes

Narrator 1 and Narrator 2 step forward and begin speaking.

Narrator 1: *[to the audience]*
Have you heard the Christmas story
about the Savior sent from glory?
The angels announced His birth
by proclaiming peace on earth.

Narrator 2: *[to the audience]*
God gave His only Son
to offer salvation to everyone.
Jesus is the reason
we celebrate this season.

Narrator 1: *[to the audience]*
But we get caught up with the worldly pleasures,
Christmas shopping and hunting for treasures.
We sometimes forget the real reason to celebrate,
so we are here today to see how some people relate.

Narrator 2: *[goes to the women with shopping bags]*
Excuse me, ladies, will you tell us the reason
why you celebrate this joyous season?

Woman 1: *[to the Narrators]*
Well, the Christmas season makes me want to drop
because all I do is shop, shop, shop.
I give and give but what do I get in return?
My feelings get hurt and I still haven't learned.
I shop at Macy's and Nordstrom's and buy gifts galore
and what do I get in return? Something from the 99 cents
   store.
But let me tell you something and my word is true.
If I don't get a decent gift this year, you can bet I'm through!

NARRATOR 1: *[to the audience]*

Giving gifts and expecting gifts in return,

I can see she still has a lot to learn.

WOMAN 2: *[to WOMAN 1]*

You can buy presents for everyone you know.

But I'm number one on my list; everyone else falls below.

I treat myself to Fendi purses and Gucci shoes.

A flat screen TV—I'm giving my credit card the blues.

Don't look at me funny, I'm not selfish you see,

but I really, really have to take care of me.

NARRATOR 2: *[to the audience]*

This isn't what I thought I'd hear.

I think I need to talk to someone else about Christmas cheer.

I see a little child over there.

I'll see if he would like to share

what he knows about this season.

Hopefully he knows that Jesus is the reason.

CHILD: *[to the NARRATOR]*

My dad thinks I believe in that jolly old man with a beard

so he puts on a red suit that just makes him look weird.

Mama decorates and sings "Deck the halls with boughs of
   holly."

She says "Santa Claus is coming, so let's all be jolly."

Then I have to hurry to bed before midnight

because Santa won't come unless my eyes are shut tight.

I love this time of year and I just want to sing.

I can't wait to see the toys my dad will bring!

NARRATOR 1: *[to NARRATOR 2]*

This isn't good; it's just not right.

Why can't we find a single soul in sight

who knows the story of the Holy Child
Born to Mary so meek and mild?

NARRATOR 2: *[to NARRATOR 1]*

No need to worry, please don't fret.
Come on my friend, we can't give up yet.
Somebody has to know the Savior lives
and experience the joy His love gives.

WOMAN 3: [*walks by hurriedly with grocery bags; narrators stop her*]
I've got to hurry home. I have dinner to make.
Turkey to roast, cakes to bake.
I'll decorate the house and trim the tree.
[*Her cell phone rings.*]
My phone is ringing, who can this be?
Hello, Mama. I'm fine and you?
See you tomorrow. Yes, dinner's at two.
Sure, bring a friend because sharing is the reason
we celebrate this holiday season.

[*WOMAN 3 passes the HOMELESS MAN and gives him a quarter and then returns to being motionless.*]

NARRATOR 1: [*to the audience*]
She's getting close. Sharing is fine.
But is the real reason clear in her mind?
HOMELESS MAN: [*to the NARRATORS*]
I wish I could go to her house and eat
instead of sitting here, cold, on the street.
A warm bed, a good meal.
I've forgotten how a hot shower feels.
Families are together giving gifts of love.
I wish I could receive a miracle from above.
I heard that Jesus was born in a manger long ago.
Is He my Savior too? I need to know.
God, if You're listening, please lend Your ear.
Send me an angel to bring me warmth and cheer.
[*huddles motionless on street under old blanket*]

NARRATOR 2: [to the audience]

She gave him a quarter, her change from the store.

On a night like this, he'll need a lot more.

But maybe this man will know the Christmas story

about the Christ child and His glory.

[NARRATORS walk towards MEAN MAN. He's extremely rude.
As the man begins to speak, narrators back away from him,
looking confused and frightened by his response.]

MEAN MAN: [walks towards NARRATORS in an intimidating
manner]

Christ child? Please! Are you insane?

There's no such thing as a child born to a virgin and man.

Get out of my face with that fantasy.

I don't believe in a Savior and His grace and mercy.

Everything I have, I worked hard to achieve.

A baby sent from God? That I don't believe.

NARRATOR 1: [to NARRATOR 2]

Does the Christmas spirit still have a home?

NARRATOR 2: [to NARRATOR 1]

I'm feeling like we're in this all alone.

WISE MAN: [approaching NARRATORS]

Allow me to encourage you and tell you what I know is true.

Jesus was born to save me and you.

NARRATOR 1: [to the crowd]

Gather around, everyone, so you can hear

why we should celebrate this joyous time of year.

[Everyone comes to life and walks towards center stage. They listen intently as WISE MAN speaks.]

WISE MAN:
While Mary and Joseph were in Bethlehem
her days were completed and she delivered the Holy Lamb.
She wrapped Him in swaddling clothes and laid Him in a
   manger
because there was no room in the inn for this tiny stranger.
The angel came to the shepherds while they attended their
   sheep.
The shepherds were frightened and they jumped to their
   feet.
Then the angel told them not to be afraid.
For in the City of David, a tiny babe is laid.
They brought good tidings of great joy.
They said He was a Savior, this baby boy.
The shepherds went to Bethlehem to see this Christ child.
They told others about the Savior so meek and mild.

The wise men saw the eastward star.
They brought gold, frankincense, and myrrh from afar.
The angels rejoiced, peace on earth, goodwill toward men.
But that's not how this story ends.
This babe grew into an incredible man
and traveled throughout all the land.
Healing the sick and raising the dead;
teaching the gospel, important words He said.
He is the Son of God, some believed and some not.
His enemies grumbled and tempers got hot.

An innocent man was crucified for our sins.

Then He died, was buried, and He rose again.

God loved us so much that He gave His only Son.

A precious gift of love, Jesus is the one.

We should honor Him always and send praises up above.

Represent His sacrifice by giving gifts of love.

Rejoice and be glad for this joyous season.

Can we all agree that Jesus is the reason?

[The crowd claps and nods their heads in agreement. Even the MEAN MAN's expression has changed.]

NARRATOR 2:

Thank God, someone knows the truth!

Study your Bible for therein lies the proof

of the birth, death, and resurrection of the king.

Believe in Him and salvation He'll bring.

NARRATOR 1:

Now you've heard the story from beginning to end.

Rest assured He lives and He's coming back again.

Share the word of Jesus with everyone you know

and celebrate His birth wherever you go.

The Best Plastic Manger Scene Ever

Susan Sundwall

Summary: Everybody in the Hobble family has a piece to contribute to the manger scene, and each piece is plastic! But when the story behind each piece is told, it becomes the best manger scene the family has ever put together.

Characters:

BRIANNA—oldest sister who is a little bossy with everybody

SISSY—little sister who has a massive collection of fashion dolls

DOUG—cousin who is living with the Hobble family for a while

MOM—BRIANNA and SISSY's mother

PASTOR HAWKINS—family friend who drops by early on Christmas Eve

DAD—BRIANNA and SISSY's father

MARY

JOSEPH

SHEPHERDS

ANGELS

Setting: living room of Hobble house decorated with Christmas tree. A small table is center stage and two chairs sit stage left.

Props: dolls (baby doll, Barbie®, Polly Pocket™ doll, and G.I. Joe®); cardboard box; stuffed animals, including a dog (favorite sleep buddy of Doug), teddy bear, small stuffed or plastic lamb; shopping bag with ribbon and wrapping paper; laundry basket; basket with Easter grass; handkerchief; small Christmas tree; star ornament; plastic cross, scarf

Costumes: biblical dress for manger people, modern-day dress for Hobble family

It's Christmas Eve, and the family still doesn't have the manger scene up because they've been too busy with the secular craziness of the holiday. BRIANNA enters stage right followed by SISSY. BRIANNA stops, turns to SISSY, folds her arms across her chest, and glares at her little sister. SISSY holds her Barbie doll behind her back.

BRIANNA: That's the dumbest idea I've ever heard!

SISSY: No, it's not! *[pulls doll from behind her back and gazes at it]* This doll has the best face for Mary. Better than yours!

BRIANNA: My doll is from the early 90's. It's . . . it's practically an antique. It's a classic! *[holds up a Polly Pocket doll]*

SISSY: That's a Polly Pocket doll! You can hardly see it!

BRIANNA: *[looks at table]* Well, the table's not very big either.

DOUG: *[enters stage left carrying a cardboard box and a G.I. Joe]* Hey, cousins! Your mom sent me in here with this box so we could set up a manger scene. *[looks at girls glaring at each other]* Um, is something going on?

SISSY: Doug, she thinks—

BRIANNA: *[interrupts]* Did you ever hear of a Barbie Mary?

SISSY: I'll bet he never heard of a Polly Pocket one, that's for sure!

DOUG: Whoa! What in the world are you talking about?

BRIANNA: I have this great idea—

SISSY: Huh, some idea!

DOUG: How about this idea? *[holds out his G.I. Joe]* He can be Joseph! *[nods enthusiastically to each one as he shows doll]*

The Best Plastic Manger Scene Ever

BRIANNA: Ewwww!

SISSY: Ewwww!

DOUG: What? I think he'd be perfect. Of course he might need
different clothes.

BRIANNA: *[hands out, palms up]* No kidding, Doug. Maybe we
could use his Jeep for the donkey.

DOUG: Well, I was just trying to help.

MOM: *[enters stage right with wrapping paper, ribbon, and*

The Best Plastic Manger Scene Ever

a shopping bag] Oh, here you all are. Pastor Hawkins will be here in a little while. I hope that manger scene will be ready.

SISSY: Mom *[holds up Barbie doll],* don't you think this is a perfect face for Mary?

BRIANNA: Mom, I—

DOUG: *[looks at G.I. Joe]* Maybe I could find a plain bandana or a . . .

MOM: I'm too busy to worry about this right now.

SISSY: But Mom . . .

MOM: *[holds hands up]* You all know what a manger scene should look like, and I know you'll do a good job. Just get on with it. *[exits stage right]*

DOUG: Why are we doing this manger scene again? *[looks puzzled]*

BRIANNA: Mom loaned ours to the church.

SISSY: Yeah, the ceramic one that Mrs. Garcia made had two broken pieces when they took it out this year.

BRIANNA: So Mom loaned them ours for under the Christmas tree in the worship center.

DOUG: Oh.

SISSY: Now *we* get to make the one for our house.

DOUG: It seems like we all want to do it our own way too. Hmm . . . let's do this; we'll each raid our closets, drawers, and toy boxes to see what we can come up with. Then we'll come back here and make up a great manger scene.

BRIANNA: Hey, Doug, that might work.

SISSY: I have a little plastic lamb from Easter!

DOUG: I have a canoe that Jesus could lay in.

SISSY: That would be a lot better than a Jeep.

BRIANNA: OK, let's do it. Come on!

[BRIANNA waves her hand for them to follow her. All exit stage left. Doorbell rings offstage.]

MOM: *[offstage]* Come in!

PASTOR HAWKINS: *[enters stage right and looks around room]* Hello?

MOM: *[follows PASTOR from stage right]* Pastor?

PASTOR HAWKINS: *[turns]* Oh, hello, Mrs. Hobble. I'm sorry; I didn't mean to barge in.

MOM: That's OK.

PASTOR HAWKINS: Well, I've got some good news!

MOM: About Doug, I hope.

PASTOR HAWKINS: Yes, we've found a home for him!

MOM: Really, how wonderful! *[looks around]* Now, where did those kids go?

PASTOR HAWKINS: He's been very happy here since your sister died, hasn't he?

MOM: Yes, he has. Why don't you come with me to the kitchen? I just pulled a big pan of peppermint brownies out of the oven. We can talk about it there.

PASTOR HAWKINS: *[sniffs the air]* So that's what I smell!

MOM: The kids will smell them too. I'm sure they'll find us. *[laughs as they exit stage right]*

[The remaining cast members assemble in the aisles. MARY, JOSEPH are in the center aisle. ANGELS are side aisle right, and the SHEPHERDS and animals are side aisle left. BRIANNA, SISSY, and DOUG return stage left. They each have a shopping bag.]

SISSY: *[holds her bag up]* Ha, ha, wait'll you see!

BRIANNA: I found the most amazing things. *[rummages around in her bag]*

DOUG: Look at this! *[pulls out a plastic Easter basket with green fake grass]* Is this a manger or what? Better than a canoe.

SISSY: Kinda looks like an Easter basket to me.

DOUG: Well, if Jesus hadn't died at Easter, we wouldn't even have Christmas.

BRIANNA: Well . . . yeah.

DOUG: And this is the last Easter basket my mom ever gave me. *[looks at it and plays with the grass]*

SISSY: You know, I think it'll work just fine. I guess you really miss your mom.

DOUG: *[sighs]* I sure do.

SISSY: *[pulls a plastic lamb out of her bag]* My mom gave me this little lamb last Easter. I had just had my tonsils out and could hardly eat anything, including my chocolate rabbit! So she gave me this.

BRIANNA: We're really glad you're here with us for Christmas, Doug. *[pulls a plastic baby doll out of her bag]*

SISSY: I can't believe you still have that!

BRIANNA: It's from when I was only five. I used to talk things over with this doll before I'd go to sleep—just like a friend. And I borrowed one of Dad's handkerchiefs to wrap it up. *[wraps doll in handkerchief and holds it up]*

DOUG: Wow, that's perfect.

SISSY: OK, let's get busy.

DAD: *[enters stage right]* Wow, looks like you kids are going to town!

BRIANNA: Hi, Dad. We're setting up the manger scene.

DOUG: Hi, Uncle Joe. We're using all our own stuff too.

DAD: What happened to our regular manger scene?

SISSY: Mom loaned it to the church.

DAD: Why did she—

BRIANNA: *[interrupts]* Long story.

DAD: OK, well I'm sure you'll do a great job. Do I smell peppermint brownies? *[lifts head and sniffs air, exits stage right]*

SISSY: *[pulls plastic star out of her bag]* We need a star for the top of the stable. I made this last year at Vacation Bible School.

BRIANNA: Oh no!

DOUG: What?

SISSY: What?

BRIANNA: We need a stable!

MOM: *[enters stage right with plastic laundry basket]* Have any of you seen your father?

DOUG: Perfect, Aunt Helen!

MOM: What?

DOUG: That laundry basket. It's the perfect thing for a stable.

MOM: *[looks at basket]* This old thing?

BRIANNA: Sure, Mom. Just leave it to us. It's perfect.

SISSY: Perfect. And dad went after the peppermint brownies.

MOM: He must have come in when I went to the garage. Pastor Hawkins is here too.

SISSY: Don't let him back in here until we're done!

MOM: OK. I'll pour him some coffee. *[exits stage right]*

DOUG: What have we got? What do we need?

BRIANNA: *[points to items as she counts them off on her fingers]*

Stable, check! Manger, check! Animals, check! Star, check! Lamb, check! Baby Jesus, check!

Sissy: Mary and Joseph—still missing! Not checked!

Brianna: Doug, I think the G.I. Joe in different clothes would be a great Joseph.

Sissy: Me too!

Doug: *[pulls already dressed G.I. Joe out of his bag]* I think you're right!

Brianna: *[turns to Sissy]* And I guess we could dress Barbie for Mary.

Sissy: *[smiles sweetly and takes already dressed Barbie out of her bag]* I was hoping you'd say that!

[Brianna, Doug, and Sissy arrange the manger scene inside the plastic laundry basket and stand back.]

Sissy: I love it!

Doug: *[nods]* Not too bad.

Brianna: Great job, everybody! Let's go see if there are any peppermint brownies left. *[exits stage right, followed by Doug and Sissy]*

Congregational Song: "It Came upon a Midnight Clear"

[As the congregation sings the song, the Angels come down. Mary and Joseph follow the Angels and sit in the two chairs on stage. Mary has baby Jesus in her arms. All remain quiet. When the story characters re-enter, they take no notice of the 'real' manger characters.]

MOM: [*enters with beautiful scarf and drapes it over the stable*] There, that looks a little better. [*looks around room*] This feels so peaceful. [*exits stage right*]

DAD: [*enters with plastic cross, hold it up and lays it on table*] There! If it weren't for Easter, we wouldn't even have Christmas. [*looks around room and smiles*] I love Christmas. [*exits stage right*]

Congregational Song: "O Little Town of Bethlehem" (first verse)

PASTOR HAWKINS: [*enters stage right*] Wow! This looks great.

BRIANNA: [*enters stage right*] It does look nice, doesn't it? Mom told me the great news about Doug.

PASTOR HAWKINS: Yes, it looks like he'll be staying right here with you.

DOUG: [*bursts in stage right*] Wahoo! Yay! I can hardly believe it.

BRIANNA: I guess Mom told him too.

SISSY: [*runs in and hugs DOUG*] You get to stay! You get to stay!

MOM: [*enters stage right*] He sure does!

DAD: [*enters stage right*] Isn't that great?

PASTOR HAWKINS: It all worked out beautifully, just like your manger scene.

BRIANNA: Pastor, will you read the Christmas story for us?

PASTOR HAWKINS: I'd be happy to.

[*PASTOR reads Luke 2:1-14 as all story characters gaze at the plastic manger. ANGELS and SHEPHERDS sing "Away in a Manger."*]

DOUG: Even though this manger scene is plastic, it feels so real to me.

BRIANNA: I was thinking the same thing.

SISSY: Sort of like the first Christmas must have been.

DOUG: The baby Jesus didn't have a home either, just like me.

BRIANNA: Until one was made for Him, and you, by a good mom and dad.

PASTOR HAWKINS: And now we know that Jesus will make a home in every heart if we let Him.

MOM: That's right.

DAD: You know what this is? *[spreads hands to show whole scene]* This is the best plastic manger scene ever!

MOM: Let's sing "Silent Night."

[PASTOR HAWKINS instructs the audience to join them in singing "Silent Night."]

Appearing of the Light

Sharon Lessman

Summary: After many years of waiting and hoping, a grandfather and his eager grandson are among the first to worship Jesus and give thanks for the light He brings to the world.

Characters:

NATHAN—10- or 11-year-old grandson of GRANDFATHER JACOB

GRANDFATHER JACOB—wise older gentleman

4 OR 5 ANGEL VOICES—male or female, mixed ages, with lines spoken offstage

CHOIR—singing "Angels We Have Heard on High" offstage

Setting: rooftop of a small house in the fields outside of Bethlehem. The skit begins at evening time and dims into night. An area is needed in a different part of the stage for the manger, which will have an unseen light (flashlight) streaming from it.

Costumes: biblical robes for GRANDFATHER JACOB and NATHAN

Props: various baskets for the rooftop, manger with straw in it, flashlight to be put inside of manger

Running Time: 10 minutes

GRANDFATHER JACOB and NATHAN are walking and talking together. They may walk down an aisle or walk around the stage as they carry on their conversation.

NATHAN: When will the light appear, Grandfather Jacob? Haven't we been waiting for it a long time?

GRANDFATHER JACOB: *[with a slight chuckle]* Nathan, I can't count the number of times you've asked that question! We must be patient and have faith in the promise that the angel spoke.

NATHAN: Tell me the prophecy again. I like hearing those words, no matter how many times you tell it.

GRANDFATHER JACOB: *[taking a deep breath, with a far-off look in his eyes]* I remember the night well. I had gone up to the rooftop to catch a cool breeze. As I was gazing into the heavens, I caught a glimpse of something very bright that seemed to be hurtling straight toward me out of the black velvet sky. I fell to the ground in fear, shielding my eyes from the brilliance. A voice began speaking, almost singing, in pure beautiful tones. I dared to uncover my eyes just a bit to catch sight of the most glorious creature I had ever hoped to see.

NATHAN: *[interrupting]* It was the angel, wasn't it, Grandfather?

GRANDFATHER JACOB: Yes, it was the angel—a bearer of light, sent to bring good news. He spoke these words to me: "You and your people have walked in darkness for many years, with little hope in your hearts. You have dwelt in the shadow of death since you rejected God himself long ago. But God has not forgotten you. I bear His words of hope to you this day. God says to you: 'I have heard the cries of your heart and have seen your pain. Lift up your eyes, for I will send you my light, born as a baby, to be with you forever. His name shall be called Jesus, the Light of Life, Dispeller of Darkness. So keep faith and hope alive as you watch and wait for my promise to appear.'"

NATHAN: How I would have loved to see that angel too.

GRANDFATHER JACOB: *[putting his hands on Nathan's shoulders]* I'm sure you would have, Nathan. With the end of the message, the angel was gone and all was still and very dark again. I sat up on the roof for a long time, thinking about how much God must love us to be willing to send His own light into this cold world of darkness. Then I repeated the words of the prophecy over and over again so I wouldn't forget them.

NATHAN: *[with awe and respect]* And you haven't forgotten them, Grandfather. I think that the Lord chose well to share His message with you! Can we go up to the roof one more time tonight? Please *[pulling at his grandfather's sleeve]*, please?

GRANDFATHER JACOB: Very well, Nathan, we'll search the skies once again for the light that was promised to us.

[NATHAN and GRANDFATHER JACOB move to another part of the stage and sit down among some baskets. Lights dim.]

GRANDFATHER JACOB: *[after a short pause]* Nathan, I feel a warm glow in my heart tonight. I think that this could be the night of the appearing of the light.

NATHAN: *[hugging his knees to his chest]* Do you think so, Grandfather Jacob? Do you really think it could be?

[Lights dim further. NATHAN falls asleep on GRANDFATHER JACOB's shoulder. The manger can be brought onstage while the two are sleeping.]

GRANDFATHER JACOB: *[after a pause for sleeping, gently shakes Nathan to wake him up]* Nathan, Nathan, wake up! Look . . . look over that hill and tell me what you see.

NATHAN: *[standing up, rubbing his eyes, hands cupped as if searching the landscape]* Do you mean that tiny dot of light?

GRANDFATHER JACOB: Yes, that tiny pinpoint of brilliance that is piercing the darkness for miles around.

NATHAN: *[pointing excitedly]* That's it! It must be the birthplace of Jesus. We must go there, Grandfather, we must go there now!

Appearing of the Light

[The two take off running or walking fast to a different part of the stage or down an aisle.]

NATHAN: *[laughing]* Grandfather Jacob, I didn't know you could move so fast! It's like you have wings on your feet.

GRANDFATHER JACOB: See how the light grows brighter as we get closer, Nathan! Look, the light is coming from that manger.

[The pair reach the light shining from a manger, and they fall to their knees. There is a pause of silent worship. GRANDFATHER JACOB then reaches out a hand toward the manger as if grasping the baby's finger.]

GRANDFATHER JACOB: *[lifting his eyes to Heaven]* Lord, now let me live in peace, for my eyes have seen Your salvation, Your promise come to pass. You have sent Jesus, Your very own light to bring life and light to all who believe in Him.

[Bring lights back up to bright as ANGELS or CHOIR speak or sing offstage. GRANDFATHER JACOB and NATHAN raise their hands in praise to God and begin to speak or sing with the ANGELS or the CHOIR.]

SPEAKING ANGELS: Glory to God in the highest! Glory to God in the highest and peace to His people on earth. He is pleased with them. Praise be to God, the light has come. Jesus is born!

[Similar phrases are joyfully repeated again and again.]

[**ANGEL CHOIR** sings "Angels We Have Heard on High."]

[After the ANGELS *are finished,* GRANDFATHER JACOB *and* NATHAN *lower their hands and take one last look at the manger, then turn to leave.]*

NATHAN: Remember the glow you felt in your heart earlier tonight, Grandfather?

GRANDFATHER JACOB: Yes.

NATHAN: Well, I feel it too! And I can see light shining on your face and in your eyes!

GRANDFATHER JACOB: *[laughing]* And on yours, my child. Jesus has come, God's very own Son, to shine with the everlasting light, and we shall walk in darkness no more.

GRANDFATHER JACOB and **NATHAN:** *[together, facing the audience]* In the beginning was the Word, and the Word was with God, and the Word was God. In Him was life and that life was the light of all. The light shines in the darkness and the darkness shall never overpower it. *[from John 1:1-5]* Glory to God in the highest!

Through a Starry Window

Kayleen Reusser

Summary: The magi who followed the star in the east found a
king and gave us examples of how to follow God.

Characters:

NARRATOR

3 WISE MEN

KING HEROD

Setting: night (spotlight on NARRATOR)

Props: Bible, ancient form of telescope, magi gifts

NARRATOR: *[reads from Bible]* "After Jesus was born in
Bethlehem in Judea, during the time of King Herod, magi
from the east came to Jerusalem and asked, 'Where is the
one who has been born king of the Jews? We saw his star
in the east and have come to worship him.'" *(Matthew 2:1,
2) [Wise man comes onstage and peers through telescope at
the sky.]* Far away to the east of Bethlehem, an astronomer
called a magus looked at the sky. It was his job to study
the heavens and reveal its signs to the people of his land.
Wait! What was that? A comet? *[A light in the form of a star
appears at the top of the stage.]* To the astronomer's practiced
eye, the appearance of a new comet revealed a great mystery.
It was a possible sign of God's long-awaited promise that the
Messiah was coming.

The magus had good reason to be happy. Four centuries
had passed since God had spoken through His prophets.

Some of God's people thought He had forsaken them. Their sufferings and prayers to Him must have seemed meaningless and empty.

Somehow the language of the night revealed to the astronomer and other magi who saw the same comet that a king had been born. *[Two other magi come on stage; all three look at the star.]* We don't know how they came to this conclusion. Nor do we know from the Bible account how many of these eminent men made the pilgrimage to Bethlehem. They may have come from the same district or met at a common place before traveling together to wherever the star led them.

The magi took gifts along with them. *[The magi pick up fancy gifts and move in same direction as star.]* The star led them over the hills and through valleys towards Bethlehem. But as they drew near to the city, the heavenly guide suddenly disappeared. *[Star light goes out; spotlight back on* NARRATOR.*]*

The magi had no choice but to seek information regarding the birthplace of the new king. They stopped in Jerusalem. They thought those people must have heard of the birth of the new king.

When news reached Herod and his people of the arrival of the magi, he requested an audience with them.

We don't know why there was a break in the star's guidance

to the magi. But after their visit to the palace where they informed King Herod of what they had seen and were looking for, the Bible tells us the magi rejoiced because the star suddenly reappeared. It guided them on what would be the final stage of their journey.

The magi found their baby king just as they had hoped. God sent the star to guide the magi to the king.

God still wants to guide our lives today. God is never indifferent to those who want to follow Him. Trust His leading this Christmas and know He loves you.

[Lights out.]

Poems

A Thanksgiving Song

Lorena E. Worlein

O give thanks unto the Lord.
Come and worship at His throne.
Lift your hearts and voices high
unto God, and God alone.
For His blessings full and free
given so abundantly,
humbly kneel before the Lord.
May He ever be adored.

O give thanks unto the Lord
for His goodness to all men.
For the gifts He does bestow,
bring your grateful hearts again.
For His bounty from on high,
for the gifts He does supply,
for His mercy and His love,
O give thanks to God above.

*[Can be sung
to the tune of
"Come, Ye
Thankful
People."]*

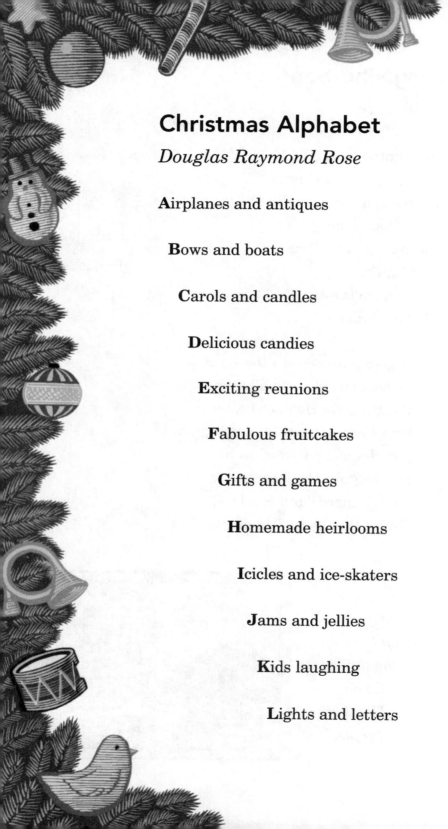

Christmas Alphabet

Douglas Raymond Rose

Airplanes and antiques

Bows and boats

Carols and candles

Delicious candies

Exciting reunions

Fabulous fruitcakes

Gifts and games

Homemade heirlooms

Icicles and ice-skaters

Jams and jellies

Kids laughing

Lights and letters

Messiah music

Nostalgic memories

Ornaments and orchestras

Pictures and poinsettias

Quiet cathedrals

Recipes and reindeer

Snowflakes and stockings

Traditional trees

Uncles and aunts

Vacation and travel

Winter wonderland

Xylophones

Yuletide chatter

Zippy zithers

Poems

Baby Jesus, We Worship You

Tammy Nischan

Baby, so tender, so precious and small,
lying so sweetly in a manger stall.

Do You hear the cattle? Do You hear the sheep
as You lie there so peacefully in a deep sleep?

Does Your Father above whisper words in Your head,
like "Sleep, my sweet Son, there is big work ahead"?

Or do memories of Heaven dance in Your dreams,
angels singing, golden sidewalks, light in bright streams?

What are You thinking, precious baby, tonight
as You enter this world with few visitors in sight?

We worship You, baby, with praises we sing!
As a man You'll become our Savior and King!

Thank You, dear little one, for coming to earth
so that we all can have a chance of rebirth!

Come to the Manger

Lois Rotz

Come with me to the manger
and see the Christ child lay,
snuggled so warm and comfy
on His bed of hay.

Hear how the cattle are lowing
in tones that are soft and sweet
as they welcome the gift sent
   from Heaven,
and little Lord Jesus they greet.

Hope Sees a Star

Douglas Raymond Rose

The wise men waited patiently,
seeking divine signs from afar.
In the midst of the darkest night—
HOPE sees a star!

The shepherds too lay sleeping,
then saw angels from afar.
In the midst of the blackest night—
HOPE sees a star!

In spite of voiceless doubts and fears,
no matter what problems there are.
Look up in spite of life's dark night—
HOPE always sees a star!

Keeping Watch

Douglas Raymond Rose

Shepherds kept watch that first Christmas—
their wide eyes fixed on high skies
as herald angels soon appeared—
that glorious first Christmas night.

I too must keep watch for Jesus,
not just once, but every day,
for soon He'll return to the earth
to take His faithful bride away.

Keeping Christ in Christmas

Douglas Raymond Rose

Let us keep Christ in Christmas.
Do it now without delay.
He's the real reason for the season.
He's the life, the truth, the way.

Let us keep Christ in Christmas.
Sing praises to Him most high.
In the City of David a Savior is born:
King Christ—great king of might.

Christmas Potpourri

Douglas Raymond Rose

Take a dash of excitement.
Add some cinnamon too.
There's really just no telling
what this delicious aroma can do.
Add some bayberry candles
and plenty fresh pinecones too.
Simmer by a red cozy fire.
Add some cheery children too.
Mix with the myrrh of kindness.
Add some frankincense of joy.
Release your Christmas potpourri.
Inhale prayerfully—and enjoy!

The Best Gift

Douglas Raymond Rose

Amid all the Christmas baubles,
amid all the jingling silver bells,
may you find the Christ of Christmas—
in spite of all the holiday sales.

Amid the colorful paper wrappings,
there's one gift that is best;
it's the greatest gift of Jesus Christ—
He's the best of all the rest!

What I Like

Darlene Mitchell

I like to get lots of gifts under the Christmas tree.
I like bikes, games, or even my favorite DVD.
I like to eat a big Christmas dinner.
I like turkey, cakes, and pies; they're always winners.
I like to stay up late on Christmas Eve night.
I like to try and peek in the packages, but they are
    wrapped too tight.
I like to go to church and sing Christmas songs of joy.
I like to read in the Bible about Mary's baby boy.
I like to hear that Jesus loves even a child like me.
I like knowing that He is my Savior and He sets the
    captives free.
I like knowing that I am God's child, an heir to the
    heavenly throne.
I like knowing that one day I'll be with Him
    in my heavenly home.

Thank you for using this program book. To serve you better, we would like to know what you think of it. We invite you to fill out this evaluation and mail, fax, or e-mail your comments to us. We truly appreciate your time and help!

Standard Publishing, Attn: Program Book Editor, 8805 Governor's Hill Drive, Suite 400, Cincinnati, OH 45249, 513-931-0950 (fax), Christmas@standardpub.com (e-mail)

As a whole, this program book was
❏ very helpful   ❏ OK   ❏ not helpful

I would like to see more   ❏ dramas   ❏ skits   ❏ plays   ❏ poems
        ❏ readings   ❏ readers' theater   ❏ monologues
        ❏ programs   ❏ ideas for services   ❏ other:

I would like to see fewer   ❏ dramas   ❏ skits   ❏ plays   ❏ poems
        ❏ readings   ❏ readers' theater   ❏ monologues
        ❏ programs   ❏ ideas for services   ❏ other:

Please tell us why you bought this book.

What improvements or changes would you suggest for this book?

Would you like Standard Publishing to offer drama resources   ❏ for children?
        ❏ for teens?   ❏ that are topical?
        ❏ for other holidays and seasons?   ❏ other:

Do you prefer: ❏ to purchase and download drama resources from a Web site?
        ❏ to purchase drama resources in print form?

Other comments:

May we use your comments in our advertising materials?   ❏ Yes   ❏ No

Personal Info   **Church Info**
Name _____   Name of Church _____
Address _____   Address _____
City, State, Zip _____   City, State, Zip _____
Phone # _____   Church phone # _____
E-mail address _____   Church denomination and size _____

Gender: ❏ Female   ❏ Male

Age: ❏ 18–24   ❏ 25–34   ❏ 35–44   ❏ 45–54   ❏ 55+

May we contact you through mail or e-mail?   ❏ Yes   ❏ No

If you would like to write for Standard Publishing's program books, please visit www.standardpub.com and read our writer's guidelines.